Spotlight on Reading

Compare & Contrast

Grades 5–6

Carson-Dellosa Publishing LLC
Greensboro, North Carolina

Credits

Layout and Cover Design: Van Harris
Development House: The Research Masters

Cover Photo: © 2002 Brand X Pictures

This book has been correlated to state, common core state, national, and Canadian provincial standards. Visit *carsondellosa.com* to search for and view its correlations to your standards.

Carson-Dellosa Publishing LLC
PO Box 35665
Greensboro, NC 27425 USA
www.carsondellosa.com

ISBN 978-16-099-6488-7
05-281187784

About the Book

The activities in *Compare and Contrast*, Grades 5–6, are designed to improve students' reading comprehension skills and to give them the skills necessary for finding similarities and differences in text. With a variety of fun and instructional formats, teachers can provide an introduction, reinforcement, or independent practice for this essential reading skill. To ensure a high level of interest, exercises are linked to other areas of the curriculum, such as math, science, social studies, and language arts.

Use these selections for independent practice or whole-group instruction. Have students work with partners or teams to complete the more challenging activities. Another idea is to place the activity sheets in a center and reproduce the answer key for self-checking.

• •

Table of Contents

Name _____

Look at the figures below. Write the words in the blanks.

white

red

yellow

pink

red

blue

orange

green

black

purple

black

1. The white ◯ is about the same size as the _____ ☐ .

2. The yellow ◯ is larger than the _____ ☐ .

3. List the shapes (include their colors) that are larger than the blue ☐ .

_____

_____

_____

_____

4. List the shape (include its color) that is about the same size as the pink ◯ .

_____

Same or Different?

Contrast these two pictures. List the differences between the two.

Example:

There are two craters behind the house.

I. _____

2. _____

3. _____

4. _____

5. _____

6. _____

7. _____

8. _____

9. _____

10. _____

Example:

There are three craters behind the house.

I. _____

2. _____

3. _____

4. _____

5. _____

6. _____

7. _____

8. _____

9. _____

10. _____

Is To!

Look at the figures. Circle the letter of the correct answer.

1. ▶ is to ▲ as:

    a. ⬇ is to ➡
    b. ➡ is to ⬆
    c. ➡ is to ⬅

2. ☺ is to ☺ as:

    a. ☺ is to ☺
    b. ☺ is to ☹
    c. ☹ is to ☹

3. ☐☐◻ is to ◻☐☐ as:

    a. 🐾🐾🐾 is to 🐾🐾🐾
    b. ☐ is to ☐
    c. 🐾🐾 is to 🐾 🐾

4. ★(★ is to (★(as:

    a. ☐○☐ is to ☐☐○
    b. ☐○☐ is to ○☐○
    c. ☐☐☐ is to ○○○

5. ═ is to ═ as:

    a. ⦀ is to ‖
    b. ⊟ is to ▯
    c. ═ is to ═

6. **A** is to ∀ as:

    a. **A** is to **a**
    b. **A** is to **b**
    c. **A** is to ∀

7. ⋀ is to ⋁⋁ as:

    a. ⋒ is to ⋃
    b. ⋀ is to ⋀⋀
    c. ⋃⋃ is to ⋃

8. **X** is to **Y** as:

    a. **Y** is to **Z**
    b. **B** is to **A**
    c. **X** is to **x**

Compare and Contrast • CD-104544

Name _____

Analogies compare things. Read each phrase and fill in the blank with a word that completes each analogy.

• •

1. **Chirp** is to **bird** as _____ is to **dog**.

2. **Spoon** is to **bowl** as **straw** is to _____ .

3. **Hair** is to **human** as _____ is to **rabbit**.

4. **Pencil** is to **write** as **paintbrush** is to _____ .

5. **Dry** is to **desert** as _____ is to **ocean**.

6. **Rink** is to **hockey** as _____ is to **football**.

7. **Water** is to **pool** as _____ is to **balloon**.

8. **A** is to **B** as **C** is to _____ .

Draw a picture to complete each analogy. Fill in the missing words.

9. Engineer   is to   train   as   pilot   is to _____ .

10. Hive   is to _____   as   nest   is to _____ .

Name _____

Circle the letter in front of the correct answer.

• •

1. How are desktop computers like castles?
   a. Both have drawbridges.
   b. Both have towers.
   c. Both have staircases.

2. How is using the Internet like flying?
   a. You use an airplane.
   b. You need a pressurized cabin.
   c. You can reach faraway people and places very quickly.

3. How is a CD like a rainbow?
   a. It has the colors of the spectrum.
   b. It is shaped the same.
   c. It forms in the rain.

4. How is a computer mouse like a real mouse?
   a. It moves around swiftly and quietly.
   b. It needs cheese.
   c. It has teeth.

5. How is the computer age like the time of the Sumerians?
   a. Sumerians invented computers.
   b. A new way to record information was invented.
   c. We write on clay tablets.

6. How is Web research like hunting for objects?
   a. You need to decide on a goal.
   b. You need to gather clues on the way.
   c. both a and b

7. How is surfing the Web like looking at the world from space?
   a. The print is small.
   b. It can give you a different perspective.
   c. You need a spaceship.

Compare and Contrast • CD-104544

Name _____

Here are some examples of reference books and their purposes. For questions 2–5, write the letter of the best resource book the person should use to find the information he or she is seeking. For questions 6–7, write the answers.

. . . .

Example:

What is a zither?

A. almanac: facts and information about a specific year
B. atlas: maps of regions, countries, states, and provinces
C. encyclopedia: detailed information about many topics
D. thesaurus: words and their synonyms and antonyms
E. dictionary: words and their meanings

I. She should use a/an __E__.

Where is Tierra del Fuego?

2. He should use a/an _____.

I want to know more about ladybugs.

3. She should use a/an _____.

What was the #I song on the day I was born?

4. She should use a/an _____.

What is the opposite of the word "serendipitous?"

5. He should use a/an _____.

6. What references would be most useful if you had to write a report and make a poster about China? _____

7. What references would be useful if you had to write a poem using adjectives that mean great? _____

Something Is Not Right

Read each group of words. For questions 1–7, fill in the circle in front of the item that does not belong. For questions 8–13, circle the letter in front of the word or phrase that tells what the items have in common.

1. ◯ horse ◯ beagle ◯ collie ◯ terrier
2. ◯ car ◯ truck ◯ convertible ◯ pyramid
3. ◯ George Washington ◯ Abraham Lincoln ◯ Theodore Roosevelt ◯ Danny
4. ◯ happy ◯ disappointed ◯ glad ◯ delighted
5. ◯ delighted ◯ miserable ◯ neighbor ◯ anxious
6. ◯ walked ◯ hurried ◯ crawled ◯ married
7. ◯ tail ◯ paw ◯ muzzle ◯ jeans

8. joyful miserable anxious
   a. happiness b. sadness c. emotions

9. war argument disagreement
   a. conflict b. harmony c. nation

10. hamsters cats dogs
    a. amphibians b. reptiles c. pets

11. car truck sedan
    a. dogs b. vehicles c. sandwiches

12. tail paw fur
    a. parts of a dog b. parts of a person c. parts of a car

13. muzzle snout beak
    a. noses b. ears c. eyes

Compare and Contrast • CD-104544

Name_____

Compare the following movie descriptions. Choose a movie title for each of the customers below. Write your recommendations on the lines.

• •

Animated *Adventures of Mama Llama*—For ages 2–10; Mamma Llama travels from her mountain home to the city, meeting many silly animals along the way
Comedy *The Magic Baseball*—For ages 7 and up; a young boy finds a baseball that never misses the bat, and he makes it to the World Series
Musical *Dance Until You Drop*—For ages 10 and up; a group of clumsy teenagers try to enter a dancing competition
Drama *Olden Days*—For ages 18 and up; two army veterans reflect on their childhoods in a sentimental and heartwarming story
Drama *Holiday Happenings*—For ages 7 and up; family members make a holiday happy and special
Romance *Together Forever*—For ages 18 and up; two people with different backgrounds fall in love despite obstacles from their families

 "My brother and I are sports fans!"

1. I recommend: _____

_____

 "I like upbeat movies with lots of music!"

2. I recommend: _____

_____

 "My husband and I want a film with some history."

3. I recommend: _____

_____

 "I need to keep my four-year-old twins entertained."

4. I recommend: _____

_____

 "It is our anniversary, and we want something romantic."

5. I recommend: _____

_____

Name _____

Read the letters. Then do the exercise on page 13.

- -

Dear Yena,

My name is Li Lui. I am 10 years old. I live in Beijing, China. My parents and I live in a tall apartment building. Our city has more than 10 million people. It is a busy city with crowded sidewalks and lots to do.

I like school. I attend from 7:00 A.M. until 4:30 P.M. My favorite subjects are art and Chinese. I don't like math at all, but I have to study it every day! I wear a blue school uniform that looks like a warm-up suit.

I love drawing, watching TV, and eating. My favorite shows are cartoons. My favorite food is rice. We eat a lot of rice, fish, and vegetables. We eat fish for breakfast to start the day with protein for strength. I like to drink soda.

When I grow up, I'd like to be a fashion designer. I want to design beautiful clothes for famous people to wear. Then, when I go to the movies I can say, "I created that outfit!"

I'm glad to have a pen pal from another country. I hope you are having a nice day! Please write soon.

Sincerely,
Li Lui

Dear Li Lui,

Thank you for writing! I am excited to have a pen pal from China. Your country seems exotic to me. I live in Accra, the capital of Ghana. My home is a one-floor house on a quiet street. I live with my parents and grandmother.

I enjoy school most of the time. My favorite subject is science. I want to be a pediatrician when I grow up, so I can help heal sick children. I'm not so good at French. I need to practice more, but I find it so dull! I wear a uniform to school too. It's a brown dress with a yellow shirt.

My favorite television programs are cartoons too. Maybe we watch the same shows. Do you like "Scooby Doo"? I do! I love to eat plantains. They're similar to bananas. I could eat them all day! I eat a lot of rice, also. I like fruit juice better than soda, though.

We have lots in common! I hope you are doing well, and I look forward to your reply.

Sincerely,
Yena

Pen Pals (cont.)

Fill in the webs with information from the pen pal letters on page 12. Write Li Lui's information on the left and Yena's information on the right. Draw stars next to the answers they have in common.

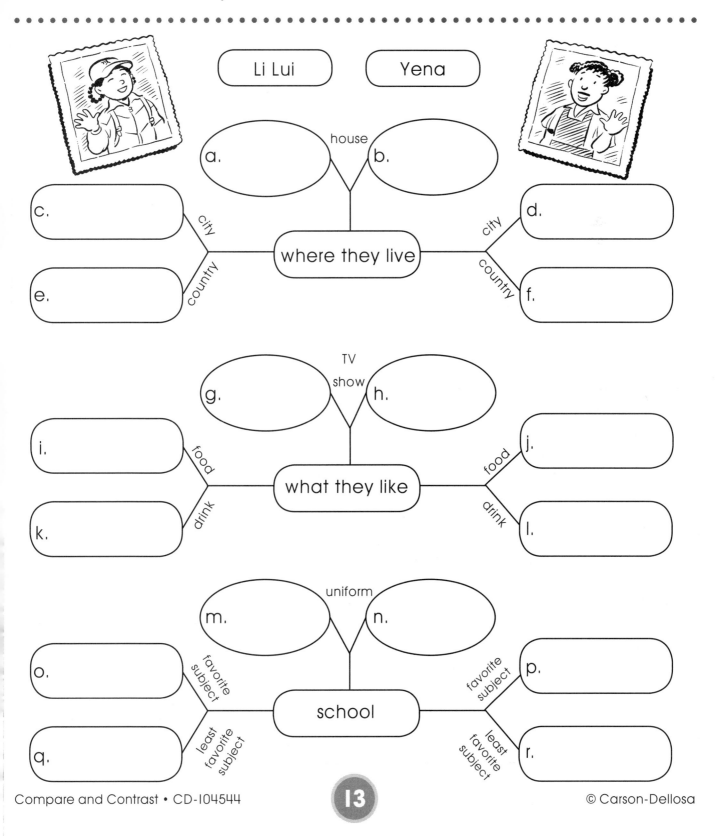

Analogies

Circle the letter in front of each correct answer.

• •

1. **Telescope** is to **star** as **microscope** is to _____ .

   a. planet   b. glass   c. cell

2. **In** is to **import** as **out** is to _____ .

   a. exit   b. exult   c. export

3. **Assertive** is to **passive** as **definite** is to_____ .

   a. vague   b. exact   c. define

4. **Evil** is to **malevolent** as **good** is to _____ .

   a. sullen   b. benevolent   c. relentless

5. **Hate** is to **detest** as **love** is to _____ .

   a. fear   b. adore   c. tolerate

6. **Reveal** is to **divulge** as **hide** is to _____ .

   a. discover   b. imagine   c. conceal

7. **Observe** is to **observation** as **condense** is to _____ .

   a. condenser   b. condensation   c. watch

8. **Gratitude** is to **ingratitude** as **grateful** is to _____ .

   a. ungrateful   b. thankful   c. gratefully

Name _____

Snow Day

Read the following poems and read each numbered statement. Write the letter **A** if the sentence applies to the first poem. Write the letter **B** if the sentence applies to the second poem. Write a **C** if it applies to both poems. Write a **D** if it applies to neither poem.

• •

A. The children awoke to a happy sight,
   While they were sleeping, the world had turned white.
   Their mother peered into their room and said,
   "No school today. Go back to bed!"

B. Father heard the news from his bed
   And pulled the pillow over his head.
   Slipping on the ice,
   Is not very nice!
   He wished it was summer instead.

1. The person is annoyed. _____

2. Someone wishes for a different season. _____

3. Winter is welcomed. _____

4. The setting is winter. _____

5. The poem takes place at midnight. _____

6. The main idea of the poem is how snow forms. _____

7. The main idea of the poem is a reaction to snow. _____

8. The person in the poem will have to get up soon. _____

9. The people in the poem can go back to sleep for as long as they like. ____

10. The poem mentions an item from a bedroom. _____

Mystery of the Missing Jam

Read the story below. Answer the questions on the next page.

· ·

"I left the jam right here on the table," said Kay, exasperated. "Now it is gone!"

Stolen!

"The bread is gone, too," said Daniel. "Hey, someone left the silverware drawer open. You know how Mom does not like that." He shut the drawer.

"The back door is not closed all the way." Kay opened the door wider. She and Daniel walked out into the backyard and looked around cautiously.

"Do you think someone came into the house?" Daniel asked, looking worried.

Kay smiled. "Someone coming into the house just to take bread, jam, and a few pieces of silverware? I do not think that is very likely." She glanced around again.

Daniel noticed a glinting object on the deck steps. "Look over there! It is one of our knives."

Kay walked down to pick it up. She looked at it closely. "Still clean," she said.

Daniel stared past his sister at the newly dug flower bed. "Somebody has been walking through all that mud." He bent down to look.

"Someone with very small feet," he added.

"Now we are getting somewhere," said Kay. "I think we both know who is behind this!" She followed the footprints, which came to an abrupt end at the edge of the flower bed.

Mysterious prints

Scanning the rest of the yard, Daniel pointed at the potting shed. There was a muddy footprint on its stone step.

Quietly, Daniel and Kay crept toward the shed. Slowly, they opened the door, knowing they would see the person inside.

Opening the door to the potting shed

When they looked inside the shed, they found Nancy sitting on the floor, her face covered with jam.

Since she had lost the knife on the trip from the kitchen, she was spreading jam on pieces of bread with her fingers.

Kay sighed. "Looks like bath time for you, kid! You're a mess."

Nancy just smiled happily and said, "Jam!"

Compare and Contrast • CD-104544

Mystery of the Missing Jam (cont.)

1. Which sibling is more observant? Circle your answer.   Kay   Daniel
   List three reasons for your choice:

   a. _____

   b. _____

   c. _____

2. Fill in the chart. Write a conclusion for each clue. Compare the clues.
   Star the clue you felt was most helpful to Kay and Daniel in solving
   the "mystery." Circle the clue that was most important in showing the
   location of Nancy.

Mystery Clues and Conclusions	
Clue	Conclusion
a. finding the knife on the deck steps	a. The person had gone down the steps.
b. a clean knife was found	b.
c. small footprints in the flower bed	c.
d. a muddy footprint on the shed step	d.

3. a. Who is the youngest? Circle your answer.   Kay   Daniel   Nancy

   b. How do you know? _____

   _____

4. a. Who do you think is the oldest? Circle your answer. Kay Daniel Nancy

   b. Why do you think so? _____

   _____

Family Differences

Look at the pictures below. Write the name(s) of each brother or sister to fill in the blanks.

Jake   Julia   Joey   Jimmy   Jessica   Jordan   Josh

1. _____ is the youngest in the family.

2. _____ has the longest hair.

3. _____ has her hair in two pig tails and Jessica's is in one pony tail.

4. _____ looks the most athletic.

5. _____ appears to read more than Josh.

6. _____ is the boy taller than Jordan.

7. _____ has the least hair.

8. _____ 's skirt is shorter than _____ 's.

9. _____ is the girl taller than the twins.

10. Julia is taller than _____.

11. _____ and _____ are of similar height and
    are not twins.

Name _____

Letter Writing

Read the chart below that describes different types of letters. Compare the letter openings. Put a **P** beneath each personal letter. Put a **B** beneath each business letter.

Business Letters	Personal Letters
Application: In this type of letter, you ask for a job.	Social: This letter is to send or accept an invitation.
Inquiry: This letter asks about an order or product.	Congratulatory: You write this to say, "Great job!"
Order: This is a letter making a purchase.	Conversational: This letter sends news to friends.
Acknowledgement: You write this letter to say you have received something that was sent to you.	Thank-you: You write this letter to thank someone for a gift, a meal, or another kind act.

Dear Sir:
I have received the web that I ordered, and I am not happy with it. It does not appear strong enough to lasso any kind of tuffet on the market. Please let me know what I need to do to ship it back to you . . .

_____

Dear Tweedledee,
Things sure are dull here without you. The Mad Hatter did say he's planning a party soon, though. The Red Queen tried to ride my motorcycle the other day . . .

_____

Dear Madam:
A friend advised me that you are looking for a nanny. I have excellent references from the Banks family, and I am able to travel via my own umbrella. However, I first need to know . . .

_____

Read the letter and then write your reply.

Dear Lucky Prize Winner:
    Congratulations! The Captain Hook Travel Agency has chosen YOU as the winner of our **"Travel One Way to Paradise"** trip. Please let us know immediately if you would like to fly away to be our honored guest at a tropical feast, featuring a genuine crocodile and other surprises!
The clock is ticking—answer today!
Your reply: _____

_____

_____

Name _____

Matter Matters

Read the following paragraph. Answer the questions.

● ●

Matter makes up everything around us. Matter takes up space and has weight. There are three states of matter: solid, liquid, and gas. Solids have a definite volume and shape. The shape of a solid is not easy to change. The small particles that make up a solid are firmly linked to each other. Liquids have a definite volume but no definite shape. They take on the shape of the container that holds them. The particles in liquids move more slowly than those of gases, and they stick together in bunches. Gases have no definite volume or shape. Their particles move very quickly and are far apart from each other.

1. Write the states of matter in order from most solid to least solid.

    a.   b.   c.

Circle the word or phrase that best fits in each of the sentences.

2. Gas particles move (faster, slower) than liquid particles.

3. A person can walk through a (gas, solid), because the particles are far apart.

4. A solid has a definite (shape, color), but a liquid does not.

5. When water is at room temperature, it (has a definite shape, does not have a definite shape).

6. When water freezes, its shape (cannot be easily changed, can be easily changed).

7. When water evaporates, it (has a definite shape or volume, does not have a definite shape or volume).

Fill in the chart below. Use examples other than the ones already mentioned above.

State of Matter	Definite Shape	Definite Volume	Example
Solid	8.	yes	9.
Liquid	10.	11.	12.
Gas	no	13.	14.

Name _____

Complete each analogy. Draw pictures to represent the analogies in questions 14 and 15.

• •

1. **Hudson** is to **river** as **Erie** is to _____ .
2. **One** is to **unicycle** as **two** is to _____ .
3. **Meow** is to **cat** as _____ is to **pig**.
4. **Racket** is to **tennis** as _____ is to **baseball**.
5. **Syrup** is to **pancake** as **frosting** is to _____ .
6. **Baby** is to **adult** as _____ is to **dog**.
7. **Jet** is to **pilot** as _____ is to **conductor**.
8. **English** is to the **United Kingdom** as _____ is to **China**.
9. **Squeak** is to **mouse** as **roar** is to _____ .
10. **Hat** is to **head** as _____ is to **foot**.
11. **Tie** is to **laces** as **zip** is to _____ .
12. **Stop** is to **go** as **begin** is to _____ .
13. **Black** is to **white** as _____ is to **day**.

14. House is to person as shell is to turtle.

	is to		as		is to	

15. Wheel is to wagon as tire is to car.

	is to		as		is to	

Fact or Opinion?

Read and identify each sentence as either fact or opinion. Circle your answer.

• •

1. Friends are the most important thing in the world.

    fact   opinion

2. Kittens are cute.

    fact   opinion

3. Santa Barbara is in California.

    fact   opinion

4. Air hockey is fun.

    fact   opinion

5. Tadpoles die without water.

    fact   opinion

6. Tadpoles turn into frogs.

    fact   opinion

7. It is always a good idea to save wild animals.

    fact   opinion

8. When there is not enough rain there is often a drought.

    fact   opinion

9. A eucalyptus is a tree.

    fact   opinion

A House Divided

Read the following paragraphs. Answer the questions.

• •

The year was 1860. The United States was about to go to war with itself. What were the problems? One major issue was slavery. Slavery existed mainly in the South. Slaves worked on large farms. In the North there were not as many farms. Slavery was not permitted in the North. People who tried to outlaw slavery were called **abolitionists**. One group from the North wanted slavery to be illegal in the United States.

Another problem between the North and the South was the way people made money. The North wanted high **tariffs**. Tariffs are taxes charged by the federal government for goods imported into the country. The North had more people and was wealthier than the South. The money from tariffs contributed greatly to projects like new railroads for the North. New railroads were making the North rich.

The Southern states were more rural. They were dependent on farm crops and not industries. The South wanted low tariffs in order to keep selling cotton to other countries like England. The South felt that low tariffs would continue to encourage trade between the U.S. and other countries. High tariffs would put a burden on other countries who wanted to trade with the U.S.

The South wanted stronger states' rights. Then each state could make its own laws. Lincoln was the new president. His Republican party was on the side of the North.

Write an **S** on the line following each phrase or statement that describes the South. Write an **N** on the line following each phrase or statement that describes the North.

1. wanted high tariffs _____
2. new railroads _____
3. stronger states' rights _____
4. mostly farms _____
5. slave labor _____
6. abolitionists _____
7. industrial _____
8. depended on crops _____

9. Contrast how the North and the South felt about stronger states' rights as opposed to being subject to federal laws. _____

_____

_____

Career Day

It is Career Day at the space station! Professionals have set up booths with information about their jobs. Compare information. Answer the questions on page 25.

· ·

Accountant

Description: Keeps track of financial records at space station. Records intergalactic sales.
Pay: 6 million zlotz
"I use my computer skills and like working with numbers. I'm handling the money of the stars!"

Flight Attendant

Description: Goes on intergalactic flights, serves meals, and helps travelers.
Pay: 1 million zlotz
"I get to meet people from many places. I have to be calm in emergencies . . . like when the microwave quits."

Librarian

Description: Catalogs books and multimedia materials from all galaxies and universes.
Pay: 3 million zlotz
"I love to recommend new holograms and virtual-reality titles to people."

Software Designer

Description: Creates and maintains all software that runs the space station.
Pay: 10 million zlotz
"My job is important. If a program has a bug in it, you get lima bean juice instead of stellar cola in the Orion Cafeteria."

Flying Saucer Mechanic

Description: Repairs flying saucers and other craft.
Pay: 2 million zlotz
"If you don't want to be lost in space, you need someone like me on your station team!"

Career Day (cont.)

1. Which job is **most** dependent on being good with people?

   _____

2. Which job requires the **most** computer knowledge?

   _____

3. Circle the best word to complete each sentence.

   a. A person who is good with numbers might be a/an
      (accountant, flight attendant).

   b. A person who likes to read might choose to be a/an
      (accountant, librarian).

   c. A person who wants to be home to greet his or her children after
      school every day might choose to be a (mechanic, flight attendant).

   d. A person who wants to create something to help people and make lots
      of money might choose to be a/an (accountant, software designer).

4. Here are three other jobs at the space station. Circle the one you would
   like best. Write your reasons on the lines below.

Cafeteria Cook
"Slinging that hyper-hash all day takes a lot of stamina!"

Galactic Educator
"I love teaching children from all universes."

Translator
"Can you speak Zordex? How about Twangie? I can speak both!"

_____

_____

_____

_____

25

Racket Sports

Read the following paragraph to complete the activity. Fill in the chart comparing the two games on page 27. Some phrases will be used twice.

• •

Tennis is played on a flat, rectangular area called a court. Usually the courts are found outside. In cold or inclement weather, indoor courts may be available. Tennis is played with either two players (singles) or four players (doubles). A tennis court's size is the same for singles and doubles. The court's boundaries are marked with white lines on its floor. A net, which stretches across the middle of the court, divides the court in half. There is a forecourt and a backcourt on each side of the net. Players on either side of the net hit the ball back and forth. Tennis is played with a strung racket and a hollow rubber ball covered with a fuzzy cloth. Only four points are needed to win a game.

Squash is played indoors on a four-walled court. Red lines are painted on the floor and walls of the court to show the boundaries. A different sized court and a different ball are used for singles and doubles. The singles' ball is soft and hollow. The doubles' ball is hard and hollow. Players use strung rackets to hit the ball against the four walls. In order to win, one side must win 15 points.

Name _____

usually outdoors	two or four players
red boundary lines on court and walls	four
hit ball back and forth across net	strung
soft and hollow (singles)	flat, rectangular
hit ball against walls	always indoors
hollow rubber ball covered with fuzzy cloth, hard and hollow (doubles)	net stretched across court
four walls	15
	hit ball against four walls

	Tennis	**Squash**
Court	a.	b.
Racket	c.	d.
Ball	e.	f.
Points to win	g.	h.
How game is played	i.	j.

At the Dog Show

Contrast the information in the following paragraphs. Complete the activity on page 29.

Sporting dogs are often used by hunters. They are good at tracking both lost things and other animals. Some examples are Labrador retrievers, English setters, and spaniels. Sporting dogs make very good pets, but they do need a lot of exercise.

Hounds are natural hunters. They have a keen sense of smell and catch other animals. Beagles, dachshunds, and greyhounds are hounds. These breeds are some of the most ancient of dog breeds.

Working dogs have been bred for a variety of jobs. They are sled dogs, guard dogs, herding dogs. Boxers, Saint Bernards, Doberman pinschers, collies, German shepherds, and sheepdogs are in this group. They are popular because of their loyalty and their even tempers.

Terriers can dig tunnels and dive into holes after badgers or foxes. These small dogs are scrappy and fearless. But, they are also quite playful. Airedales, schnauzers, and Scottish terriers are examples.

There are *toy* breeds of dogs that love to sit in people's laps. They are so cute, they look like animated toys. They are smart, alert, and often noisy! Chihuahuas, pugs, and Shih Tzus are toys.

Nonsporting dogs do not seem to fit into any of the other dog groups. Bulldogs, dalmatians, and poodles fall into this group. The poodle is the exceptionally smart. The dalmatian is the mascot for firefighters. And bulldogs are slobbery, affectionate friends.

At the Dog Show (cont.)

At the dog show, some of the dogs have run away! Help these owners find their dogs. For descriptions 1–6, draw a line from each statement to the possible place the dog may have gone. Write your answer to question 7.

1. "Titan is such a huge Doberman. I can't imagine that he could have gone far without someone seeing him!"

2. "Dots is a sweet Dalmatian. At work, you hardly even notice her."

3. "Angus is what we call our Scottish terrier. He must be around here somewhere!"

4. "Our Destry is as beautiful as Lassie. Where could she be?"

5. "Someone could have stepped on Bits! He's the smallest pug I've ever seen!"

6. "Max, our Labrador, is gone! Where should we look for him?"

digging a tunnel

guarding a house

sitting on someone's lap

herding sheep

sleeping at a firehouse

retrieving ducks

7. How are sporting dogs and hounds similar? _____

_____

_____

Two Boys, Two Cultures

Read the following paragraphs. Use the lines under each paragraph to take notes. Answer the questions on page 31. Circle **True** or **False** to answer each question.

• •

Alfred is a member of the Zulu tribe. He and his family live in rural South Africa. They live in a mud house. There is no electricity in the house. The family uses candles and oil-burning lamps. A common meal in Alfred's home is cornmeal mush called **iphalishi**. For dessert, there is pumpkin pudding. Meat is expensive, so Alfred rarely has it. Chicken is a special treat. It is very hot and dry in South Africa. Alfred wears shorts, even in the winter. Alfred wears a uniform when he goes to school. He learns reading, writing, English, and math, among other subjects. When he grows up, he hopes to work in the city and earn many **rands**.

_____

_____

_____

_____

_____

Ivan lives in urban Russia. His family lives in an apartment with three rooms. Ivan's family owns a radio and small television. A common meal for Ivan is pancakes and bread. Meat is expensive, but chicken is a special treat. It is often very cold and windy in Russia. In the winter there is a lot of snow. Ivan wears a school uniform and attends third grade. He learns reading, writing, math, and English. When he grows up, he wants to be an engineer and earn many rubles.

_____

_____

_____

_____

_____

Two Boys, Two Cultures (cont.)

1. Both Alfred and Ivan like to watch television.   True   False

2. A typical meal for both boys includes food made
   from grain.   True   False

3. Meat is expensive for both Alfred's and Ivan's families.   True   False

4. Both Alfred and Ivan use money called **rands**.   True   False

5. Both boys wear uniforms to school.   True   False

6. Alfred likes chicken, but Ivan does not.   True   False

7. Ivan wears shorts in the wintertime.   True   False

8. Ivan and Alfred both live in the country.   True   False

9. **Iphalishi** is a special Russian dish.   True   False

10. Both Alfred and Ivan want to work and earn money
    when they are adults.   True   False

Name _____

Read the following descriptions of these important members of the government in the Fairy Tale Kingdom. Answer the questions on the next page.

• •

Mother Goose's Cabinet is made up of fairy-tale veterans chosen by Mother Goose herself. The cabinet members' roles are to give advice based on their experience and to help run the government. Compare the job descriptions and answer the questions on the next page. Predict what Mother Goose character will be the best for the job.

The Members of the Cabinet:

A. **The Secretary of the Treasury**—Jack Beanstalk, who has the job of making sure the goose keeps laying those golden eggs. He also is in charge of the money and taxes paid in the kingdom.

B. **The Secretary of Defense**—Rumpelstiltskin, whose riddle keeps all invading armies at a standstill. He is also responsible for the kingdom's army.

C. **The Attorney General**—Puss in Boots, who is the most persuasive cat in the kingdom. He oversees the court and prison systems.

D. **The Secretary of Agriculture**—Chicken Little, who keeps track of food and crops for the entire kingdom despite various disasters. She is responsible for better crops and aid to farmers.

E. **The Secretary of Labor**—Cinderella, who is a strong advocate of workers' rights. She encourages them to leave jobs where the bosses are unkind. She helps people find better jobs and provides job training.

F. **The Secretary of Housing**—The Big Bad Wolf, who tests new housing construction himself. He sees to it that all homes are in good condition.

G. **The Secretary of Transportation**—The Cow Who Jumped over the Moon, who is also in charge of the space program. She sees that transportation is safe, whether it is beanstalk-climbing or broom-riding.

H. **The Secretary of Education**—Goldilocks, who learned a lot about character education when she made amends after being charged for breaking-and-entering the home of the three bears. She is in charge of the kingdom's school systems and training young children to respect others' property.

I. **Secretaries of the Environment**—Hansel and Gretel, who keep the kingdom free of cockroaches looking for crumbs. They also protect against water and air pollution and too many crumbs from candy and gingerbread.

Mother Goose's Cabinet (cont.)

Write the letter of the Mother Goose cabinet member who would handle each issue best.

_____ 1. Dealing with prison overcrowding

_____ 2. Introducing a new math program in schools

_____ 3. Creating laws making sure all workers are fairly paid

_____ 4. Launching a new space shuttle

_____ 5. Encouraging better air-quality practices

_____ 6. Reducing the number of flying broomsticks

_____ 7. Reviewing taxes to make sure they are fair

_____ 8. Making sure each new cottage is safe

_____ 9. "Help! Our village blacksmith just cut 10 jobs!"

_____ 10. "Our well water tastes odd. Perhaps someone is trying to play a trick on us."

_____ 11. "All my kids deserve a decent new shoe for a home."

_____ 12. "Should we build our new house of brick or straw?"

_____ 13. "I want to start a small farm. What crops grow well in this area?"

_____ 14. "I want someone to make sure that our local giant is not demanding too much tax money to pay for his protection."

33

Dynamic Duo

Read the following paragraphs. Fill in the chart on page 35.

• •

Remember reading about the abolitionists of the American Civil War? They wanted to see slaves freed. They wanted them to have equal rights. Elizabeth Cady Stanton was an abolitionist. Stanton came to a World Anti-Slavery Convention in London. When she arrived, she became angry when she discovered women were not able to speak or vote at the convention.

At the convention, Stanton met other women who were also unhappy because women were not recognized at the meetings. The women planned special meetings to talk about these problems. They called their own convention to improve women's rights. The convention was held in Seneca Falls, New York. It helped to launch a movement toward equal rights for women. This movement was called women's suffrage. It sought to extend women's rights to vote, run for office, and receive fair wages.

Meanwhile, Susan B. Anthony was working to convince industries to hire and pay women equal to men. She fought for the right of women to join trade unions run by men. Stanton soon developed a working relationship with Anthony. The two made a great team. Stanton wanted to help women, but she did not want to travel. She had growing children at home. Stanton was writing speeches for Anthony to deliver across the country. Anthony was single and had no children.

The pair founded the National Woman Suffrage Association. Stanton became its president. Anthony was always the more popular and better known of the two. Her travel back and forth across the country made her familiar to many Americans. She devoted all of her efforts to women's right to vote and hold office. She is best remembered for this.

By contrast, Stanton was involved in many areas of reform for women. She did not think that the voting was any more important than the right to hold political office or own property. Elizabeth Cady Stanton's husband once said to his wife: "You stir up Susan, and Susan stirs up the world!"

Name _____

Dynamic Duo (cont.)

Below the heading called Same, list the similarities between Elizabeth Cady Stanton and Susan B. Anthony. Under Different, list the differences between the two women.

	Same	Different
Elizabeth Cady Stanton		
Susan B. Anthony		

Using the information from the chart, write two statements showing how these two ladies were a lot alike and how they were very different.

_____

_____

_____

_____

_____

Bread

Read each recipe. Use the information from the recipes to fill in the Venn diagram on the next page. Write at least three facts unique to each recipe and three facts that they share.

• •

Grilled Cheese

Lunch Item Ingredients:
2 slices of bread
1 or 2 slices of cheese
margarine or butter
one slice of ham or bacon (optional)

Directions: Butter two slices of bread. Add cheese and ham to **unbuttered side** of top slice. Place skillet on burner at medium heat. Place top slice of bread with cheese and ham in skillet, butter side down. Top with other slice, butter side up. Toast until golden brown and cheese starts to melt. Flip and toast other side. When toasted evenly, remove from heat. Cut in half and eat like a sandwich.

French Toast

Breakfast Item Ingredients:
2 slices of bread
1 egg
vanilla and cinnamon (optional)
margarine or butter
syrup

Directions: Crack egg into bowl and beat. Add 1/4 tsp. (1.2 mL) vanilla and sprinkle of cinnamon, if desired. Place pan on burner at medium heat. Dip both sides of bread into egg mixture. Lay in pan. Toast until golden brown. Flip and toast top side. When toasted evenly, remove from heat. Top with margarine or butter and syrup. Eat on a plate with a fork.

Name _____

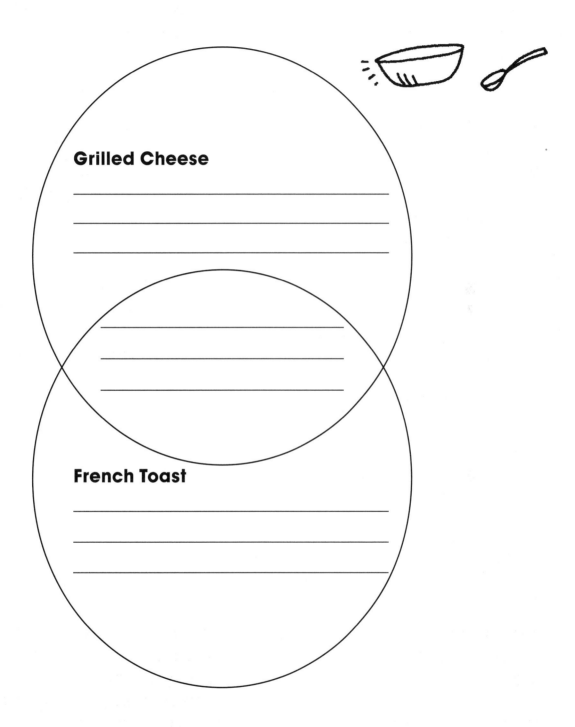

Grilled Cheese

_____
_____

_____

_____
_____

_____

French Toast

_____
_____

_____

The Great Salt Lake

Read each paragraph. Write a fact on the lines after each paragraph.
Complete the chart on page 39.

• •

1. If you have ever played in puddles of water you know you can create a lake by obstructing the water's flow with dirt or rocks. Many natural lakes form the same way. _____

   _____

2. Water can flow into a lake from one large source or from many small sources. Many mountain lakes are filled by tiny streams that trickle down from melting snow. Most natural lakes have outlets, low places where water can leave the lake. Some of the world's greatest rivers have their origins in such outlets. An outlet from Lake Victoria in Africa is the source of the Nile, the famous river that flows through Egypt. _____

   _____

3. When streams bring water into a lake and an outlet allows that water to escape, the lake stays fresh. Extra minerals and salts dissolved in the water do not remain in the lake. They are carried through the outlet and travel down to the ocean. _____

   _____

4. When river waters are blocked by natural rock or earth formations in the desert, they spread out to form a lake, just as they do in the mountains. Because there is less rain in the desert, the waters of the lake do not rise up far enough to find an outlet. Instead of flowing out of the lake, the water evaporates. It leaves dissolved minerals and salts behind. These minerals make desert lakes salty. _____

   _____

5. The Great Salt Lake in Utah is an excellent example of a desert lake. About 30,000 years ago, when there was much more rainfall in Utah, Nevada, and Idaho, The Great Salt Lake was 10 times its current size. There were no people around then, but geologists can tell from ancient shorelines and other evidence that the lake had an outlet. Its waters were fresh, not salty. Geologists have named that ancient body of water Lake Bonneville. _____

   _____

Name _____

6. Because the Great Salt Lake contains dissolved minerals from Lake Bonneville as well as minerals added by modern rivers and streams, it is too salty for most fish. Only minuscule brine shrimp, salt flies, bacteria, and algae live in the water. Much like the oceans, many birds, including pelicans, herons, gulls, and terns, live in marshes along the shore.

_____

_____

7. The salinity, or saltiness, of the Great Salt Lake varies in different years and in different parts of the lake. When there is a high level of precipitation, the water is less salty. When there is a drought, the water is saltier. The salinity of the lake varies between 9 percent and 28 percent. It is always many times saltier than ocean water, which has a salinity level of three percent. _____

_____

Use the information supplied to fill in the correct circles to complete the chart.

		Oceans	Great Salt Lake	Both	Neither
1.	salty	○	○	○	○
2.	supports many plants and animals	○	○	○	○
3.	fresh water	○	○	○	○
4.	has islands	○	○	○	○
5.	is in Utah	○	○	○	○
6.	has 3% salinity	○	○	○	○
7.	salinity varies from year to year	○	○	○	○
8.	size varies from year to year	○	○	○	○
9.	is only about 30 feet deep	○	○	○	○
10.	is in Michigan	○	○	○	○
11.	has dissolved minerals in the water	○	○	○	○
12.	loses water to evaporation	○	○	○	○
13.	is home to pelicans and gulls	○	○	○	○

Name _____

Settling the West

Read the passage and answer the questions on the next page.

• •

Pioneers helped expand America by moving to the unsettled West. Most traveled in wagon trains. Often, several families joined together in their move west. They traveled together for safety. Some hired guides to lead them along mountain trails. Others used boats where there were large rivers.

Some pioneers traveled on foot, carrying only a rifle, an ax, and a few supplies, but most went by wagon. However they traveled, they did not take many belongings. They found many food items along the way. They hunted and fished for their food. They used hides for clothing and blankets. They ate dried meats and grains that they carried with them.

The earliest settlers crossed the Appalachian Mountain in the 1770s. The wagon trains followed various trails on their way west. Southern routes went through the Cumberland Gap. This is a natural pass in the mountains of Virginia. In 1775, Daniel Boone helped open the Wilderness Road. This trail ran from northern Virginia to Kentucky. It followed buffalo trails. Native Americans had used these paths for trade and hunting along the Ohio River. Until 1775, the rough trail could only be traveled on foot or horseback.

During the next 80 years, 300,000 people used the Wilderness Road. By 1796, the road was made into an all-weather road. The road served both wagons and carriages. Today, an important highway follows much of the route.

Thousands of New England pioneers used the Mohawk Trail. This trail crossed New York and Massachusetts. It was made by the Iroquois Tribe during wars with other tribes. This trail was also important during the American Revolutionary War. It was replaced by the Erie Canal and railroads before the end of the 1800s. It followed the Mohawk River.

Pioneers were able to travel short distances in a day. Most trips took many weeks, even months. Wherever they settled, pioneers had to clear land. They lived in tents or in the wagons until they could build log homes.

Name_____

In questions 1–3, circle the letter of the correct answer. In question 4, complete a Venn diagram.

• •

1. What is the passage mainly comparing?
    a. the pioneers' belongings
    b. the pioneers' travel routes and experiences
    c. rivers
    d. parts of the country

2. Pioneers of the American West
    a. were all traveling and settling new lands.
    b. were not traveling but were building new houses.
    c. were all using wagons as they moved west.
    d. were all using the mountain trails.

3. What was true of only the Wilderness Road?
    a. It was first used by Native Americans.
    b. It passed through the Cumberland Gap.
    c. It ran along a river.
    d. It was an easy road for pioneer wagons to follow.

4. Compare and contrast modern-day travel through the mountains and pioneer travel through the mountains.

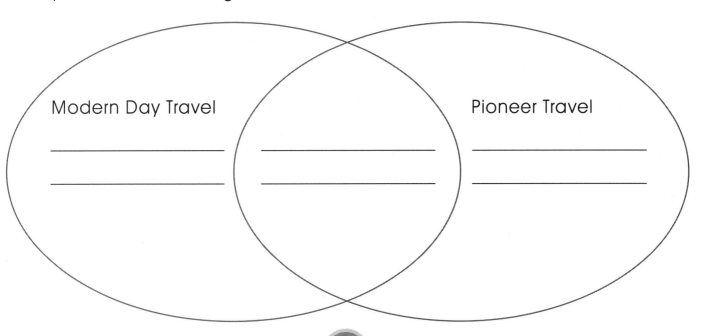

Modern Day Travel   Pioneer Travel

Name _____

Match each statement in Column A with its literal (actual) meaning in Column B by writing the letter of the correct meaning in the space. Finish the sentences at the bottom of the page with Column A statements.

• •

Column A

____ 1. It is raining cats and dogs!
____ 2. It is a dog-eat-dog world.

____ 3. He is the underdog.
____ 4. The dog days of summer
____ 5. It is going to the dogs.
____ 6. Living a dog's life

Column B

a. He is in a lesser position of power.
b. Hottest days
c. Everyone fights to get what he wants no matter the cost.
d. It is rundown and in need of fixing.
e. It is pouring.
f. Working hard and not being treated well

Column A

____ 7. Face the music.
____ 8. Keep your head above water.
____ 9. Laugh your head off.
____ 10. Head is in the clouds
____ 11. Do not lose your head!
____ 12. She is two-faced.

Column B

a. In a fantasy world
b. Take your punishment.
c. Do not become too excited.
d. Stay out of trouble.
e. Dishonest; says one thing, means another
f. Giggle hysterically

13. "These long hours are killing me!" Sue complained. "And, I get no appreciation. I'm _____

_____!"

14. "Robin is always daydreaming," the teacher commented. "Her _____

_____!"

Name _____

Kids' Computer magazine just rated the latest computer programs for students. Using the ratings chart, compare the programs. Answer the questions below.

⋯⋯⋯⋯⋯⋯⋯⋯⋯⋯⋯⋯⋯⋯⋯⋯⋯⋯

Memory Key
K stands for kilobytes: the higher the number K, the more computer memory is needed.

Rating Key

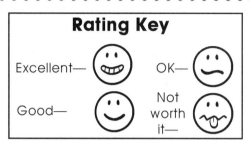

Computer Programs for Kids:

Title	Type		Rating	Comments
Exploring Under the Sea	Fantasy Adventure	320K	☺	
Taptap Typing	Educational	128K	☺	very useful
Goaltime!	Sports	512K	☺	fun soccer game
Let's Learn French	Educational	512K	☺	
Puzzlebuzz	Games	256K	☺	amazing mazes
Math Puzzles	Educational	320K	☺	
Smashtennis	Sports	384K	☺	Not a smash
Ultimate Building	Games	512K	☺	loud, worthless
Space Race	Fantasy Adventure	320K	☺	plenty of action!
Mathmagic	Educational	320K	☺	great learning tool

1. If your computer has a memory of 320 K, it cannot run any program above that number. What is the best rated program you can buy to help you with school work from the 320 K choices? _____

2. Which sports program is more highly recommended, Smashtennis or Goaltime!? _____

3. Which game program is more highly recommended? _____

4. Which fantasy adventure program is highly recommended?

_____

Compare Explorers

Read the following paragraphs. Fill in the chart on page 45.

● ●

Vasco da Gama

In 1497, King Manuel of Portugal chose a man named Vasco da Gama to sail to India. Da Gama had been a sailor since the age of 15. No one wanted to sail with Da Gama. The explorer Bartolomeu Dias had already sailed to the southern tip of Africa, called the Cape of Good Hope, but could not go any farther. The story of his trip made others not want to try again. Da Gama left on July 8, 1497. He had four ships. Four months later, he sailed around the Cape of Good Hope into new waters. The ships sailed along the eastern coast of Africa. The trip was over 11,000 miles (17,702 kilometers) long. The men were at sea for a long time. Some of them became very sick with scurvy. Scurvy is an illness that comes from not eating fresh meat or fruit. It was not an easy trip. Da Gama made it to India on May 20, 1498.

The return took over a year. When he made it home, Da Gama was a hero to his people. They gave him many riches. He was sent on two more trips to India to set up a trading post. Portugal finally had found a route to India. On his last trip, Da Gama died in India at the age of 55. During his life, he had a wife, six sons, and one daughter.

Ferdinand Magellan

In 1519, Ferdinand Magellan set sail from Spain. He had 5 ships and about 270 men. He was supposed to find a way across the Atlantic Ocean to the Spice Islands in southeastern Asia. Magellan hoped that there was a way through the American continents to Asia. When they reached South America, one of the ships decided to turn back to Spain. Magellan found a way around the southern tip of South America. He entered a new, unexplored ocean. He named it the Pacific because it seemed peaceful. But he thought that it would only take three days to traverse it. Instead, it was over 98 days before he and his crew saw land again. Most of their food was gone. Many men became very sick and died.

Finally, Magellan's crew reached the Philippine Islands on March 28, 1521. Magellan would not finish the trip he had begun. He died on the island. During his life, Magellan had a wife and two sons. The trip had taken three long years. When they crawled onto land, the men who returned became the first people ever to sail around the world.

Name _____

Fill in the chart showing the differences between Vasco da Gama and Ferdinand Magellan. Answer the questions.

· ·

Detail	Vasco da Gama	Ferdinand Magellan
Home Country		
Destination		
Traveled by		
Route		
Length of Trip		
Year of Arrival		
Family		

1. Write a sentence comparing the problems the two crews had on their voyages.

    _____

    _____

2. How did the original destination of the explorers relate to the actual place of arrival?

    _____

    _____

Answer Key

Page 4
1. green; 2. red; 3. orange square, green square, red circle, white circle; purple rectangle; 4. red square

Page 5
Sample answers: A: 1. House has three windows. 2. one planet in sky; 3. Father has moustache. 4. Father has newspaper. 5. Dog has one eye. 6. Kid has plain shirt. 7. Ball has swirls. 8. Car has two lights. 9. Scooter has no headlight. 10. Door has round window. B: 1. House has two windows. 2. two planets in sky; 3. Father is clean shaven. 4. Father has magazine. 5. Dog has two eyes. 6. Kid has striped shirt. 7. Ball has zig-zags. 8. Car has three lights. 9. Scooter has headlight. 10. Door has triangular window.

Page 6
1. b; 2. c; 3. a; 4. b; 5. a; 6. c; 7. b; 8. a

Page 7
1. bark; 2. glass; 3. fur; 4. paint; 5. wet; 6. Possible answers include: field, stadium; 7. Possible answers include: air, helium; 8. D; 9. plane; 10. bee, bird

Page 8
1. b; 2. c; 3. a; 4. a; 5. b; 6. c; 7. b

Page 9
2. B; 3. C; 4. A; 5. D; 6. encyclopedia, atlas; 7. dictionary, thesaurus

Page 10
1. horse; 2. pyramid; 3. Danny; 4. disappointed; 5. neighbor; 6. married; 7. jeans; Circled: 8. c; 9. a; 10. c; 11. b; 12. a; 13. a

Page 11
1. The Magic Baseball; 2. Dance Until You Drop; 3. Olden Days; 4. Adventures of Mama Llama; 5. Together Forever

Pages 12–13
a. apartment; b. house; c. Beijing; d. Accra; e. China; f. Ghana; g. cartoons*; h. cartoons*; i. rice; j. plantains; k. soda; l. fruit juice; m. blue; n. brown and yellow; o. science; p. art and Chinese; q. math; r. French

Page 14
1. c; 2. c; 3. a; 4. b; 5. b; 6. c; 7. b; 8. a

Page 15
1. B; 2. B; 3. A; 4. C; 5. D; 6. D; 7. C; 8. B; 9. A; 10. C

Pages 16–17
1. Daniel; a. He saw the knife first; b. He noticed the footprints; c. He saw the footprints by the shed; 2. b. The person had not used it yet. c. The person was young and/or small. d. The person was inside the shed. 3. a. Circled: Nancy; b. Sample answers: Nancy is described as little; she makes a mess; she does not realize she caused a problem. 4. a. Circled: Answers vary; Kay is likely

answer. b. Sample answers: Kay seems in charge; Daniel asks her opinion; Kay takes care of Nancy.

Page 18
1. Jake; 2. Jessica; 3. Julia; 4. Josh; 5. Jordan; 6. Josh; 7. Jake; 8. Julia, Jessica; 9. Jessica; 10 Jake; 11. Jessica, Jordan

Page 19
B, P, B; Answers will vary.

Page 20
1. a. solid; b. liquid; c. gas; 2. faster; 3. gas; 4. shape; 5. does not have definite shape; 6. cannot be easily changed; 7. does not have a definite shape or volume; 8. yes; 9. Possible answer: rock; 10. no; 11. yes; 12. Possible answer: juice; 13. no; 14. Possible answer: helium

Page 21
1. lake; 2. bicycle; 3. oink; 4. bat; 5. cake; 6. puppy; 7. train; 8. Chinese; 9. lion; 10. shoe or sock; 11. zipper; 12. end or finish; 13. night; 14. Pictures should reflect analogy; 15. Pictures should reflect analogy.

Page 22
1. opinion; 2. opinion; 3. fact; 4. opinion; 5. fact; 6. fact; 7. opinion; 8. fact; 9. fact

Page 23
1. N; 2. N; 3. S; 4. S; 5. S; 6. N; 7. N; 8. S; 9. Sample answer: Individual states could keep more control over issues like slavery and tariffs.

Pages 24–25
1. flight attendant; 2. software designer; 3. a. accountant; b. librarian; c. mechanic; d. software designer; 4. Answers will vary.

Pages 26–27
a. flat, rectangular; usually outdoors; b. red boundary lines on court and walls; always indoors; c. strung; d. strung; e. hollow rubber ball covered with fuzzy cloth; f. soft and hollow (singles); hard and hollow (doubles); g. four; h. 15; i. two or four players, net stretched across court, hit ball back and forth across net; j. four walls, hit ball against four walls

Pages 28–29
Lines drawn to: 1. guarding a house; 2. sleeping at the firehouse; 3. digging a tunnel; 4. herding sheep; 5. sitting on someone's lap; 6. retrieving ducks; 7. They are both good hunters.

Pages 30–31
1. False; 2. True; 3. True; 4. False; 5. True; 6. False; 7. False; 8. False; 9. False; 10. True

Pages 32–33
1. C; 2. H; 3. E; 4. G; 5. I; 6. G; 7. A; 8. F; 9. E; 10. I; 11. F; 12. F; 13. D; 14.

Pages 34–35

Answers will vary but should include some of the following: Same: fought for women's rights, founded the National Woman Suffrage Association, Different: Stanton stayed home while Anthony traveled, Stanton wrote speeches and Anthony gave the speeches. Stanton worked in many areas of reform while Anthony concentrated on voting. Anthony was better known than Stanton.

Pages 36–37

Grilled Cheese: uses cheese; uses ham or bacon (optional); butter bread before cooking; cut in half; eat like sandwich; French Toast: uses syrup; uses vanilla and cinnamon (optional); top bread with butter after cooking; eat on plate with a fork; Both: uses bread; uses margarine or butter; place on burner at medium heat; toast on one side and flip to toast on the other side

Pages 38–39

Paragraphs: Answer will vary, depending on facts selected.
Chart: 1. both; 2. oceans; 3. neither; 4. both; 5. Great Salt Lake; 6. oceans; 7. Great Salt Lake; 8. Great Salt Lake; 9. Great Salt Lake; 10. neither; 11. both; 12. both; 13. both

Pages 40–41

1. b; 2. a; 3. b; 4. Answers will vary but could include: Modern Day Travel: faster, cars, food purchased at stores, use highways; Pioneer Travel: slower, wagons, traveled in groups, used trails, hunted and fished for food; Both: crossing mountains, follow rivers, use boats for travel

Page 42

1. e; 2. c; 3. a; 4. b; 5. d; 6. f; 7. h; 8. j; 9. l; 10. g; 11. i; 12. k; 13. living a dog's life; 14. head is in the clouds

Page 43

1. Mathmagic; 2. Goaltime!; 3. Puzzlebuzz; 4. Space Race

Pages 44–45

Home Country: Portugal, Spain; Destination: India, Spice Islands; Traveled by: 4 ships, 5 ships; Route: Africa, South America; Length of Trip: 1 year, 3 years; Year of Arrival: 1498, 1521; Family: wife and 7 children, wife and 2 sons; 1. Sentences will vary but should include: Both crews suffered severe losses due to disease. 2. Vasco da Gama really did arrive in India while Magellan did not reach the Spice Islands but did travel around the world.